First World War
and Army of Occupation
War Diary
France, Belgium and Germany

58 DIVISION
Divisional Troops
291 Brigade Royal Field Artillery
4 October 1915 - 6 February 1916

WO95/2995/4

The Naval & Military Press Ltd
www.nmarchive.com
Published in association with The National Archives

Published by

The Naval & Military Press Ltd

Unit 10 Ridgewood Industrial Park,

Uckfield, East Sussex,

TN22 5QE England

Tel: +44 (0) 1825 749494

www.naval-military-press.com

www.nmarchive.com

This diary has been reprinted in facsimile from the original. Any imperfections are inevitably reproduced and the quality may fall short of modern type and cartographic standards.

© Crown Copyright
Images reproduced by permission of The National Archives, London, England, 2015.

Contents

Document type	Place/Title	Date From	Date To
Heading	WO95/2995-3		
Heading	58 Division Troops 291 Bde RFA Formerly 2/2 London Bde 1915 Oct-1916 Feb		
War Diary	Saxmundham	04/10/1915	19/10/1915
War Diary	Woodbridge	20/10/1915	06/02/1916

NO 95/2995/3

58 DIVISION TROOPS

291 BDE RFA
(FORMERLY 2/2 LONDON BDE)

1915 OCT — 1916 FEB

Box 2995

291 Bde RFA (formerly 2/2 Lon Bde) 2862

Army Form C. 2118.

WAR DIARY or INTELLIGENCE SUMMARY.

(Erase heading not required.)

Instructions regarding War Diaries and Intelligence Summaries are contained in F. S. Regs., Part II. and the Staff Manual respectively. Title pages will be prepared in manuscript.

Place	Date	Hour	Summary of Events and Information	Remarks and references to Appendices
	1915 Oct			
SAXMUNDHAM	4.	11.30 p.m.	Notification received "Usual air Craft positions will be taken up at once"	
	10. 15.		All lights extinguished - Two guns in pits manned and prepared for action -	
	5. 13.	1 am	Order received to resume normal working. -	
SAXMUNDHAM	10.15	8.0pm	Message received "Anti air craft intelligence and observation posts will be taken up at once"	
			All lights extinguished - Two guns in pits manned and prepared for action.	
		11.20 p.m.	Two explosions heard in S.W. direction.	
		11.45 p.m.	Engines of an Air Ship distinctly heard - apparently proceeding in a N.Easterly direction. after 10 minutes sound ceased.	
	14. 10.15	1.30 A.M.	Engines of two Air ships heard - One apparently travelling in a N.Easterly direction and the other in an Easterly direction from the W.	
			Guns again manned and prepared for action - After about 20 minutes sound ceased.	
		2.30am	Slight noise of Air ship heard - but soon died away. -	
SAXMUNDHAM	19. 10.15	10.45 a.m.	Message received "Zepplin has been sighted 70 miles due E of SOUTHWOLD"	
			Two guns with trails dug in were manned in HURTS HALL PARK.	
			Two " " " " " in KNODISHALL WHIN	
			Three " " " " " in HAZLEWOOD COMMON	
			No Zepplin sighted nor heard.	

COMMDG. 291st LONDON BRIGADE R.F.A.

Army Form C. 2118.

WAR DIARY
or
INTELLIGENCE SUMMARY.
(Erase heading not required.)

Instructions regarding War Diaries and Intelligence Summaries are contained in F. S. Regs., Part II. and the Staff Manual respectively. Title pages will be prepared in manuscript.

Place	Date	Hour	Summary of Events and Information	Remarks and references to Appendices
WOODBRIDGE	20. 10. 15.	8.45 pm.	Message received "Stand by"	
		9.25 pm.	" " "Take up usual outposts - Zeppelins reported over the WASH and the THAMES. Two Guns were run out to meadow adjoining BARRACK FARM - trails dug in and prepared for action.	
		12.00 midnight	Message received " Resume normal working "	

W. Mitchell

Brevet Colonel,
Commanding, 2/2nd London Brigade, R.F.A.

Woodbridge,
31/10/15.

Army Form C. 2118.

WAR DIARY
INTELLIGENCE SUMMARY.
(Erase heading not required.)

Instructions regarding War Diaries and Intelligence Summaries are contained in F. S. Regs., Part II. and the Staff Manual respectively. Title pages will be prepared in manuscript.

Place	Date	Hour	Summary of Events and Information	Remarks and references to Appendices
WOODBRIDGE.	11/11/15	6 p.m.	6th. County of London Battery arrived from TADWORTH & went into billets.	

W. Nichols
.....................BREVET COLONEL
COMMDG. 2nd LONDON BRIGADE R.F.A.

Army Form C. 2118.

WAR DIARY
or
INTELLIGENCE SUMMARY.
(Erase heading not required.)

Instructions regarding War Diaries and Intelligence Summaries are contained in F.S. Regs., Part II. and the Staff Manual respectively. Title pages will be prepared in manuscript.

Place	Date	Hour	Summary of Events and Information	Remarks and references to Appendices
WOODBRIDGE	7/12/15		Inspection by Lieut General R.C. Brownlow C.B. Commanding 1st Army on BRIGHTWELL HEATH	
	13/12/15		Inspection by Major General J.M. Brunker Inspector of R.H. & R.F.A. on BRIGHTWELL HEATH	
	29/12/15		Inspection by Brigadier General E.J. Cooper C.B. M.V.O. D.S.O. Commanding 58th (London) Division on MARTLESHAM HEATH	

WM Nicholls..........BREVET COLONEL.
COMMDG. 2/2nd LONDON BRIGADE R.F.A.

2/3rd Londn Signal R.F.A.

Army Form C. 2118

WAR DIARY
or
INTELLIGENCE SUMMARY
(Erase heading not required.)

Place	Date	Hour	Summary of Events and Information	Remarks and references to Appendices
WOODBRIDGE	17.1.16	10.30 A.M.	Train 15. for March I B.L.C. Sms, 4 Ammunition Wgns, 105 Horses, 2 Officers & 07 N.C.O's & men of the 2/6th Battery — & 4 G.S. Wgns, 16 Mules & 10 N.C.O's & men of the Signal Co. Ammunition Column proceeded to ORFORD by Light Rly= R.H. Kitchen, DCOLi Comdg. 2/3rd Londn Signal R.F.A.	

Army Form C. 2118.

WAR DIARY

INTELLIGENCE SUMMARY

(Erase heading not required.)

Instructions regarding War Diaries and Intelligence Summaries are contained in F. S. Regs., Part II. and the Staff Manual respectively. Title pages will be prepared in manuscript.

Place	Date	Hour	Summary of Events and Information	Remarks and references to Appendices
	1916 FEB			
WOODBRIDGE	6.			
	2.			
	16.	1 pm.	2 Officers, 87 N.C.O's & Men, and 103 horses of the 2/6th Battery - 3 G.S. Wagons, 16 Mules and 10 N.C.O's & Men of the Brigade Ammunition Column arrived from ORFORD on completion of duty as Depot Battery.	

R.F. Nixon
Brevet Colonel,
Commanding, 2/2nd London Brigade, R.F.A.(T.F.)

2353 Wt. W3544/1454 700,000 5/15 D. D. & L. A.D.S.S. Forms/C. 2118.

www.ingramcontent.com/pod-product-compliance
Lightning Source LLC
Chambersburg PA
CBHW081514160426
43193CB00014B/2690